Gorillas

by Helen Frost

Consulting Editor: Gail Saunders-Smith, Ph.D.

Consultant: Jane T. R. Dewar, Founder,
Gorilla Haven,
Morganton, Georgia

Pebble Books

an imprint of Capstone Press
Mankato, Minnesota

Pebble Books are published by Capstone Press
151 Good Counsel Drive, P.O. Box 669, Mankato, Minnesota 56002
http://www.capstone-press.com

Copyright © 2002 Capstone Press. All rights reserved.
No part of this book may be reproduced without written permission
from the publisher. The publisher takes no responsibility for the use of any
of the materials or methods described in this book, nor for the products thereof.
Printed in the United States of America.

1 2 3 4 5 6 07 06 05 04 03 02

Library of Congress Cataloging-in-Publication Data
Frost, Helen, 1949–
    Gorillas / by Helen Frost.
    p. cm.—(Rain forest animals)
    Includes bibliographical references (p. 23) and index.
    Summary: Simple text and photographs present the lives of gorillas that live in rain forests in Africa.
    ISBN 0-7368-1192-3
    1. Gorilla—Juvenile literature. [1. Gorilla.] I. Title.
QL737.P96 F76 2002
599.884—dc21   2001004844

Note to Parents and Teachers

The Rain Forest Animals series supports national science standards related to life science. This book describes and illustrates gorillas that live in tropical rain forests. The photographs support early readers in understanding the text. The repetition of words and phrases helps early readers learn new words. This book also introduces early readers to subject-specific vocabulary words, which are defined in the Words to Know section. Early readers may need assistance to read some words and to use the Table of Contents, Words to Know, Read More, Internet Sites, and Index/Word sections of the book.

Table of Contents

Gorillas 5
The Rain Forest 11
What Gorillas Do 15
Where Gorillas Sleep 21

Words to Know 22
Read More 23
Internet Sites 23
Index/Word List 24

4

Gorillas are large apes.
Apes are mammals.

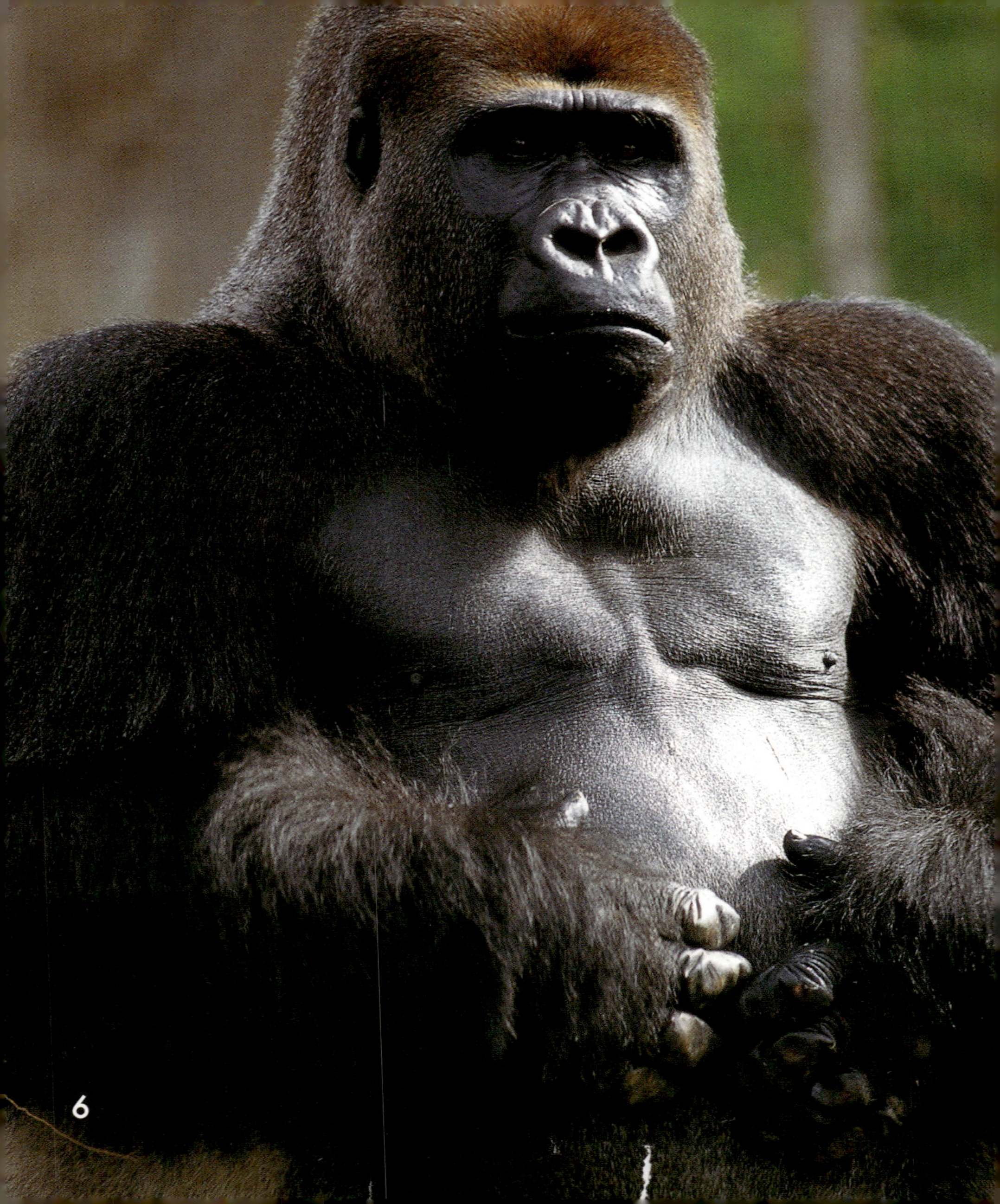

Gorillas are strong.
They have dark hair.

8

Gorillas have long arms and short legs.

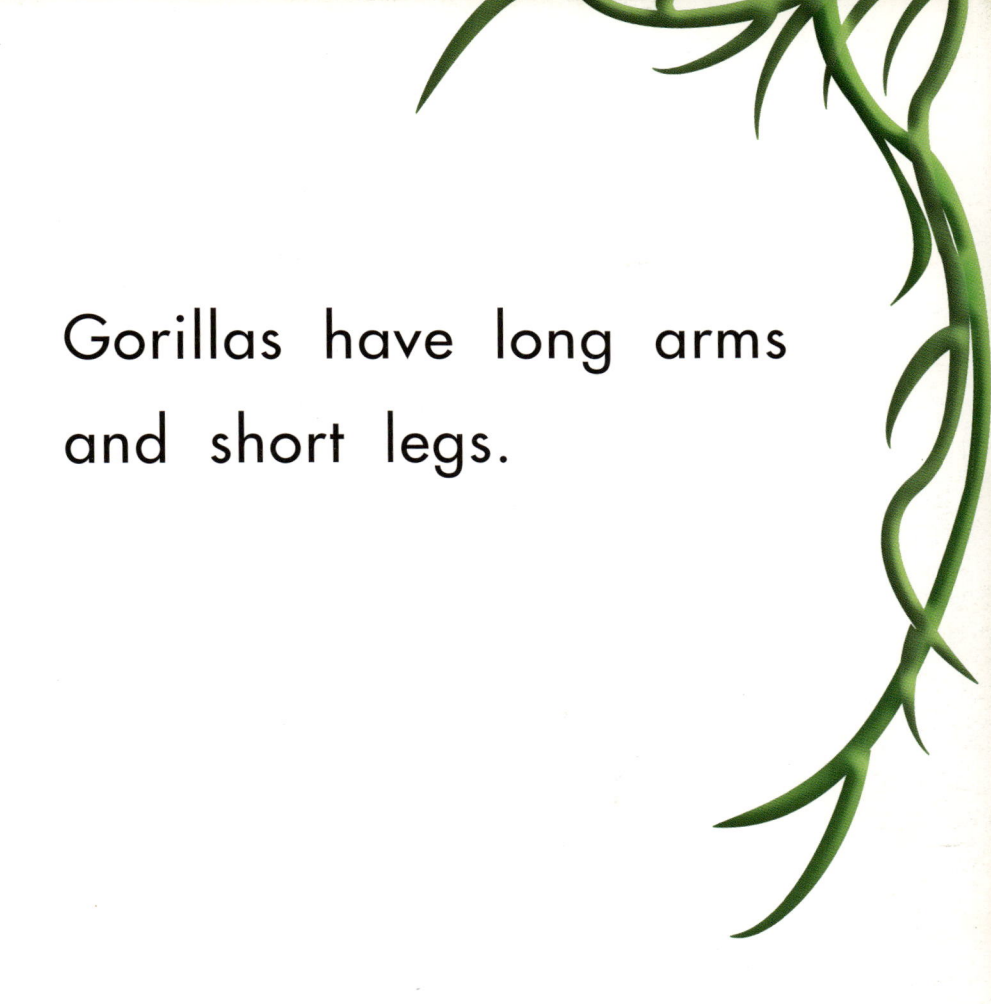

places gorillas live

Gorillas live in tropical rain forests in Africa.

emergent layer

canopy layer

understory layer

forest floor

Gorillas travel across the forest floor. They sometimes climb to the canopy layer to find food.

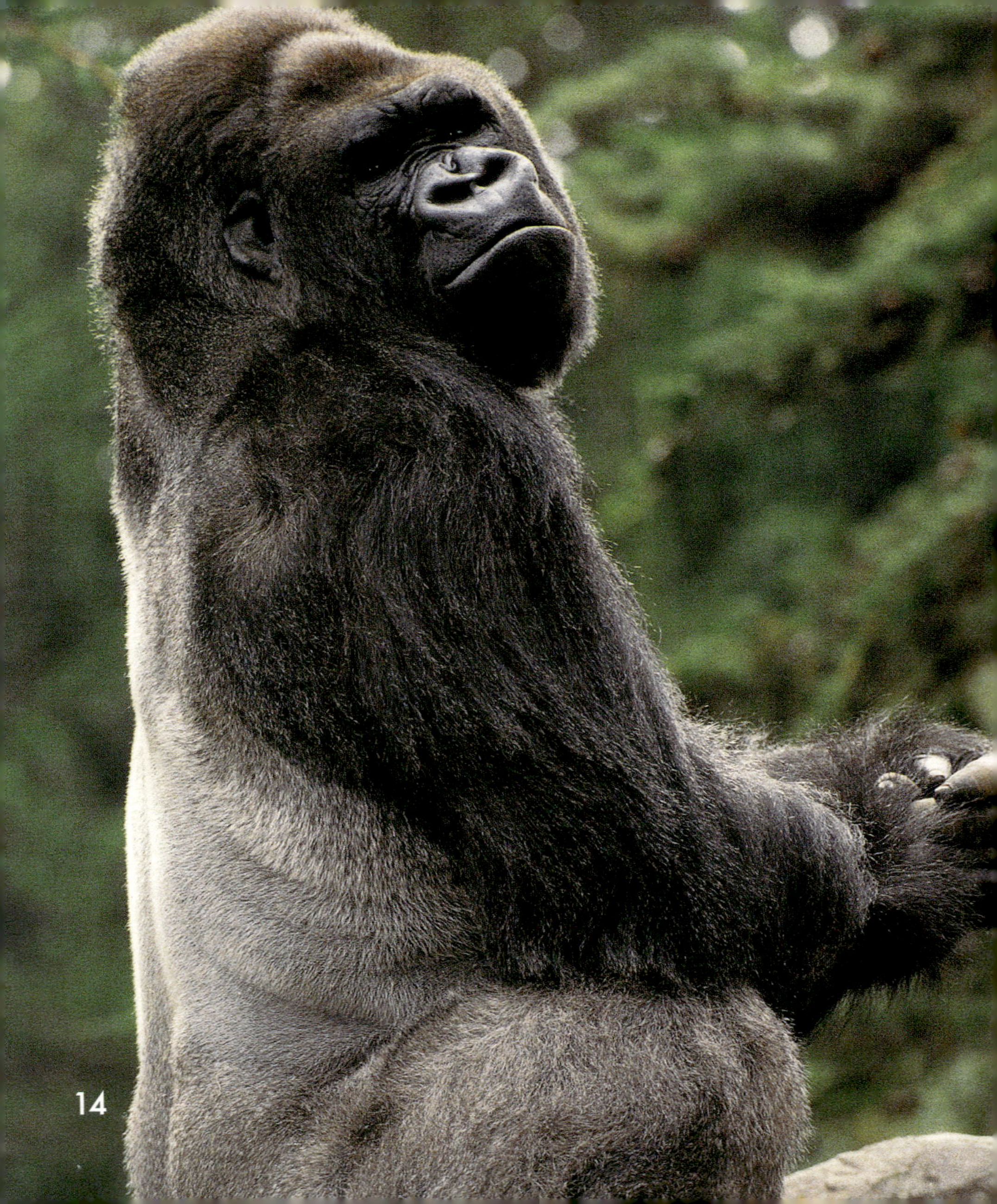

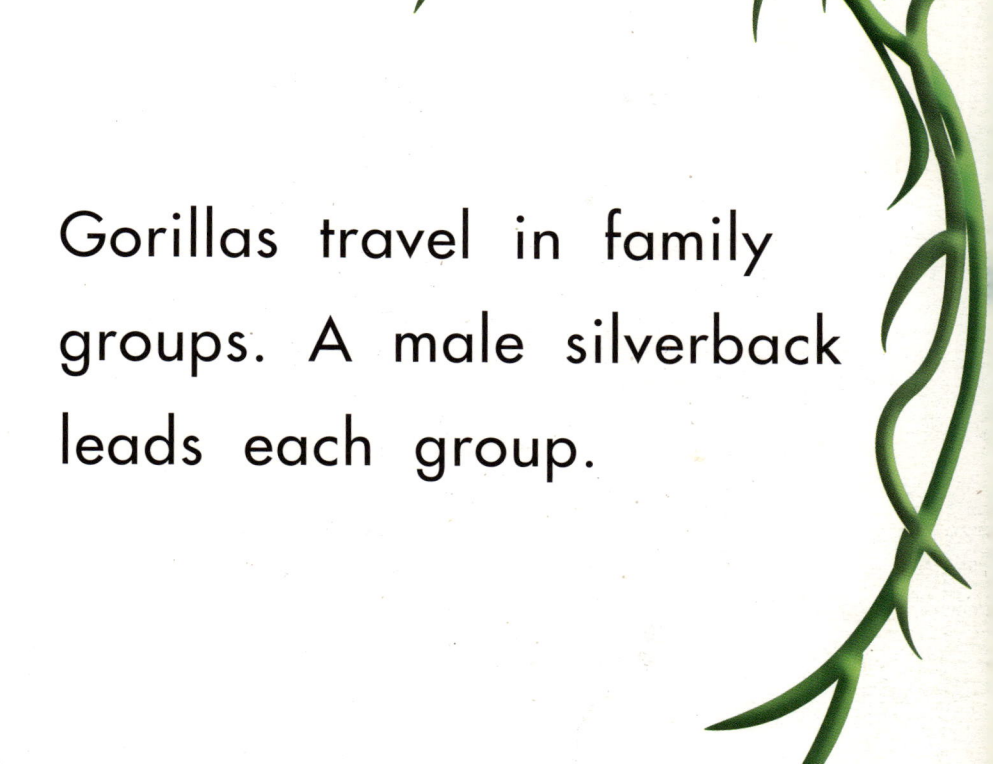

Gorillas travel in family groups. A male silverback leads each group.

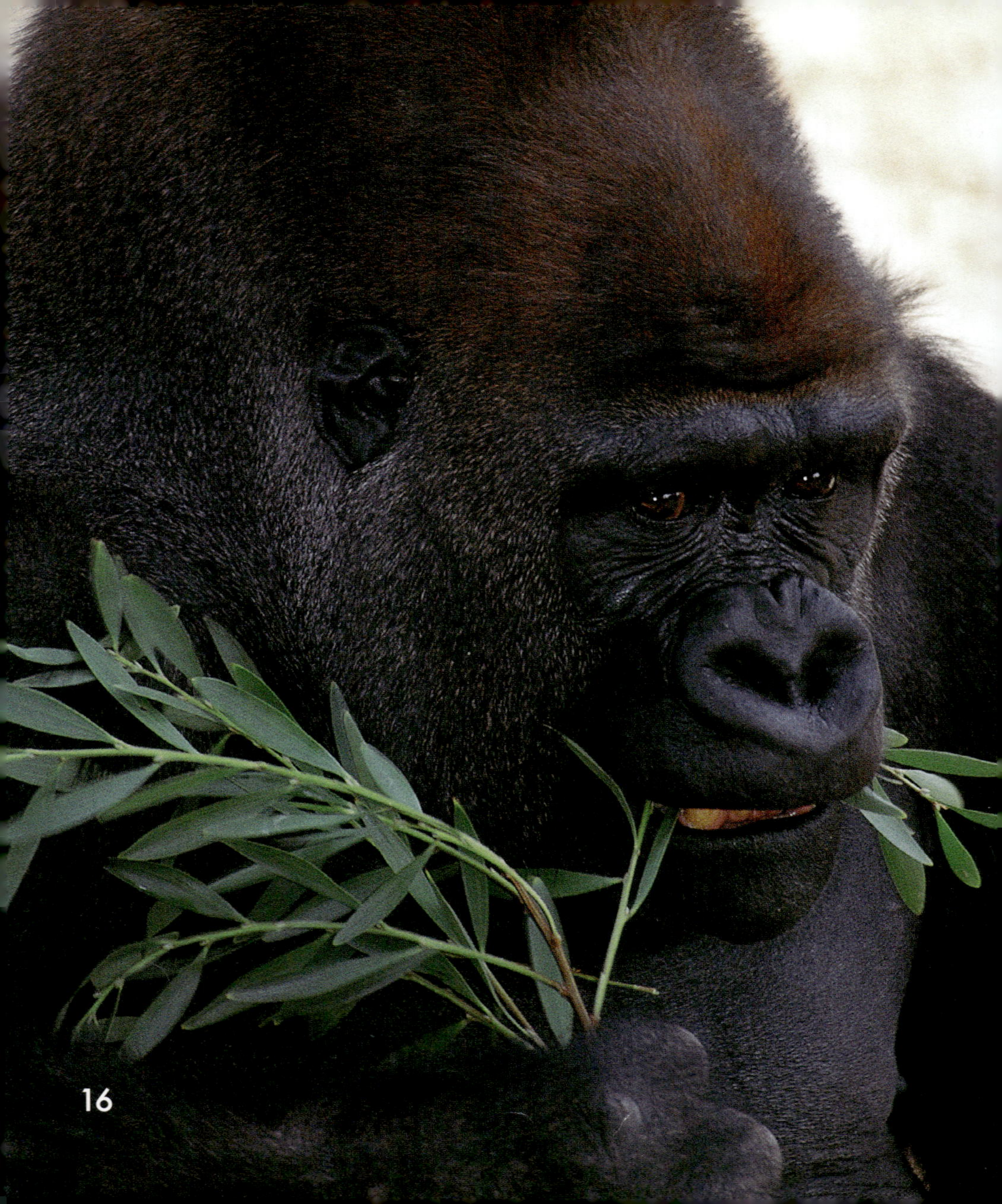

Gorillas eat plants.

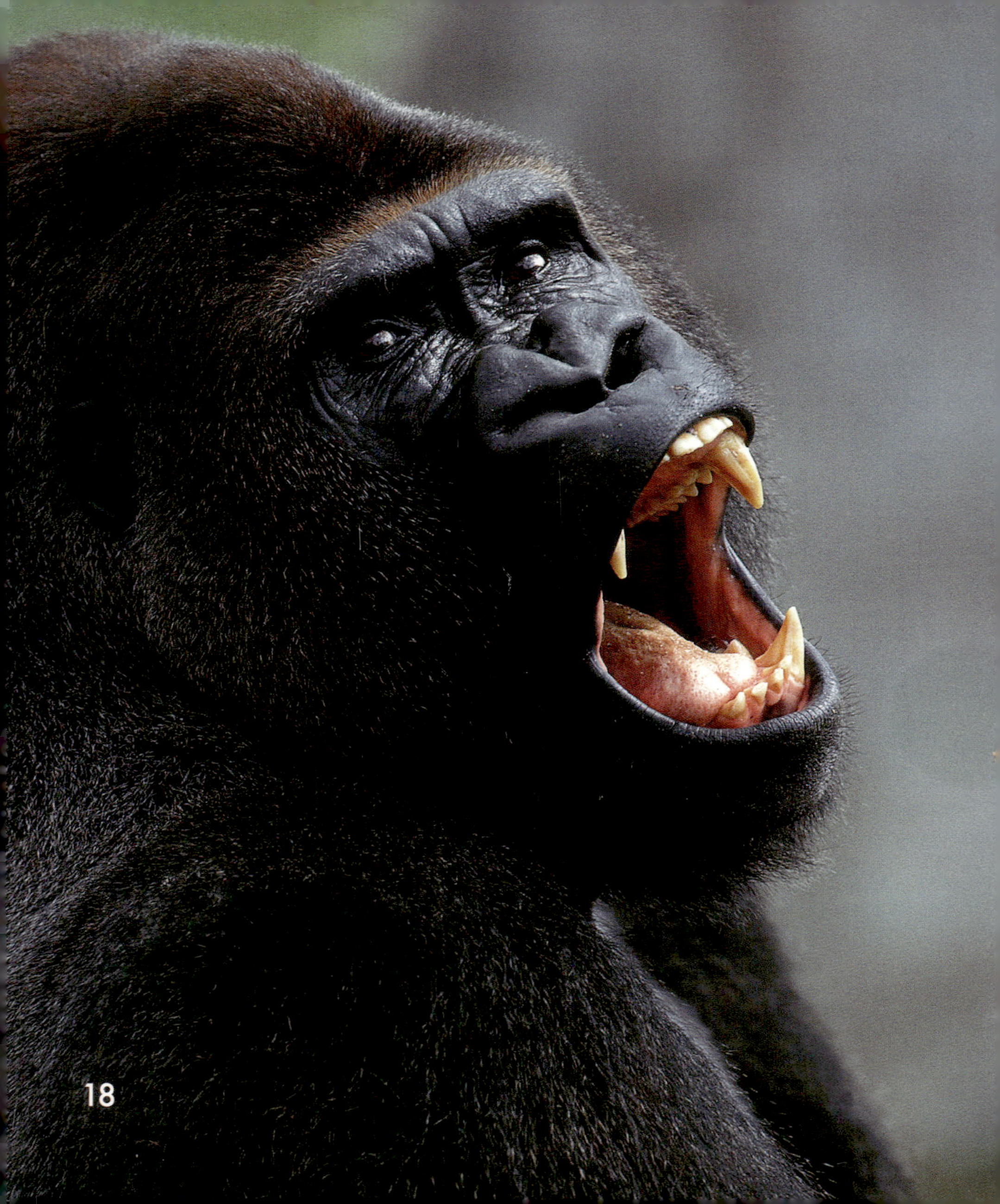

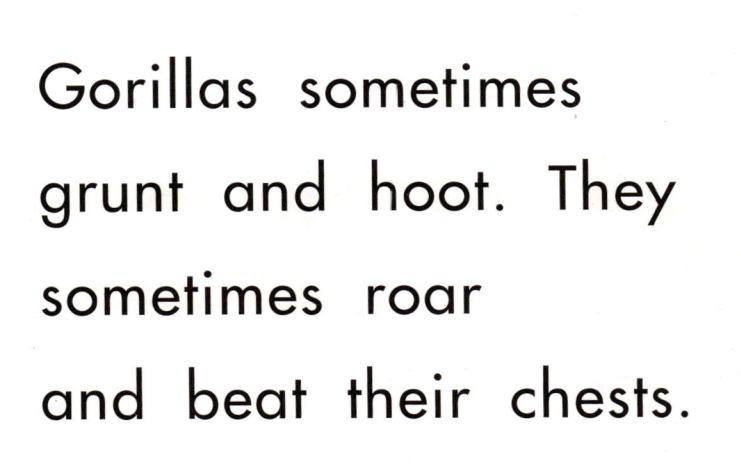

Gorillas sometimes grunt and hoot. They sometimes roar and beat their chests.

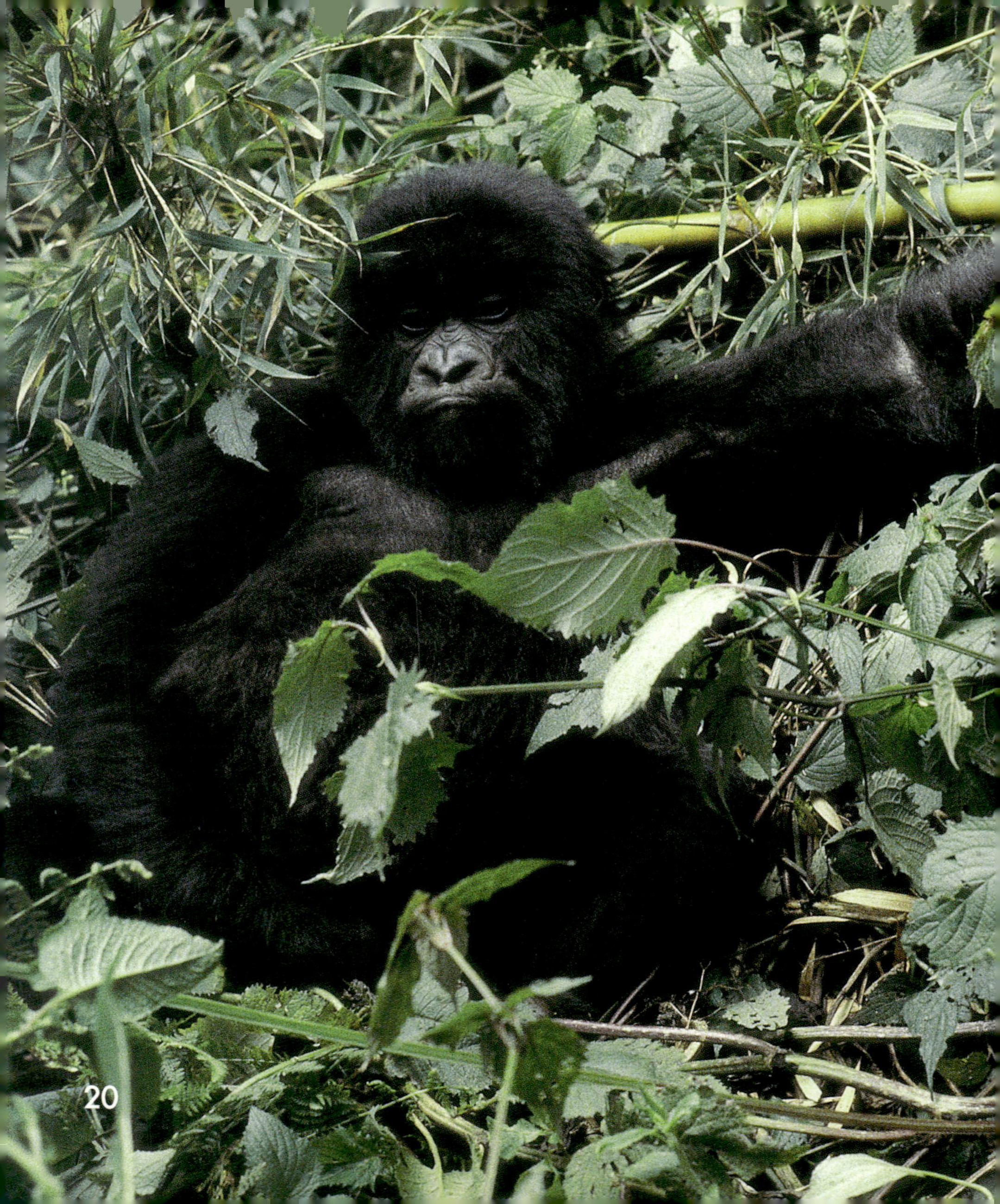

Gorillas sleep in nests.
They build new nests
every night.

Words to Know

ape—a large primate with no tail; gorillas, orangutans, and chimpanzees are kinds of apes.

canopy—the layer of treetops that forms a covering over a rain forest

male—a person or animal that can father young as an adult; some male gorillas weigh more than 400 pounds (181 kilograms).

mammal—a warm-blooded animal with a backbone; mammals have hair or fur; female mammals feed milk to their young.

nest—a cozy place or shelter; gorillas use branches and leaves to build nests; they build their nests on the ground or in trees.

roar—to make a loud, deep noise; gorillas roar and beat their chests to scare away other animals; gorillas purr and rumble when happy.

silverback—an adult male gorilla with silver-gray hair on his back

tropical rain forest—a dense area of trees where rain falls almost every day

Read More

Johnston, Marianne. *Gorillas and Their Babies.* Zoo Life Book. New York: PowerKids Press, 1999.

Martin, Patricia A. Fink. *Gorillas.* A True Book. New York: Children's Press, 2000.

Simon, Seymour. *Gorillas.* New York: HarperCollins, 2000.

Internet Sites

All About Gorillas
http://www.enchantedlearning.com/subjects/apes/gorilla

Dian Fossey Gorilla Fund International
http://www.gorillafund.org

Gorilla Haven
http://www.gorilla-haven.org

Koko's Kids Club
http://www.koko.org/kidsclub

Index/Word List

Africa, 11
apes, 5
arms, 9
canopy
 layer, 13
chests, 19
climb, 13
dark, 7
eat, 17

family, 15
food, 13
forest
 floor, 13
groups, 15
hair, 7
legs, 9
male, 15
mammals, 5

nests, 21
plants, 17
rain
 forests, 11
roar, 19
silverback, 15
sleep, 21
strong, 7
travel, 15

Word Count: 81
Early-Intervention Level: 12

Editorial Credits
Martha E. H. Rustad, editor; Jennifer Schonborn, production designer and interior illustrator; Linda Clavel and Heidi Meyer, cover designers; Kia Bielke, interior illustrator; Kimberly Danger and Mary Englar, photo researchers

Photo Credits
Digital Visions, 10
International Stock/Mark Newman, 6
James P. Rowan, 1, 8
Joe McDonald/TOM STACK & ASSOCIATES, 18
Mark Allen Stack/TOM STACK & ASSOCIATES, cover
Photo Network/Mark Newman, 4
Visuals Unlimited/Ken Lucas, 14, 16; Gerald and Buff Corsi, 20

The author thanks the children's section staff at the Allen County Public Library in Fort Wayne, Indiana, for research assistance.